T0195816

Only
by
Grace

A KINGDOM MESSAGE

Anne Sanders Grace

WESTBOW
PRESS®
A DIVISION OF THOMAS NELSON
& ZONDERVAN

WestBow Press books may be ordered through booksellers or by contacting:

WestBow Press
A Division of Thomas Nelson & Zondervan
1663 Liberty Drive
Bloomington, IN 47403
www.westbowpress.com
1 (866) 928-1240

Because of the dynamic nature of the Internet, any web addresses or
links contained in this book may have changed since publication and
may no longer be valid. The views expressed in this work are solely those
of the author and do not necessarily reflect the views of the publisher,
and the publisher hereby disclaims any responsibility for them.

Any people depicted in stock imagery provided by Getty Images are models,
and such images are being used for illustrative purposes only.
Certain stock imagery © Getty Images.

NASB: Unless otherwise cited scripture quotations taken from the
New American Standard Bible® (NASB), Copyright © 1960, 1962,
1963, 1968, 1971, 1972, 1973, 1975, 1977, 1995 by The Lockman
Foundation Used by permission. www.Lockman.org

MSG: Scripture quotations marked MSG are taken from THE MESSAGE,
copyright © 1993, 2002, 2018 by Eugene H. Peterson. Used by permission of
NavPress. All rights reserved. Represented by Tyndale House Publishers, Inc.

CJB: Taken from the Complete Jewish Bible by David H. Stern.
Copyright c. 1998. All rights reserved. Used by permission of
Messianic Jewish Publishers, 6120 Day Long Lane, Clarksville,
MD 21029. http://www.messianicjewish.net.

ISBN: 978-1-9736-7327-9 (sc)
ISBN: 978-1-9736-7328-6 (e)

Library of Congress Control Number: 2019912817

Print information available on the last page.

WestBow Press rev. date: 09/11/2019

To my husband, Bobbie Lee Grace, who shared his family name (Grace) with me, to our four J-birds (Jessica, Julie, Jill, Jason), and to all our precious grandchildren, I dedicate this part of my life for all you have contributed in various ways.

I love you always,

Rachel Anne Sanders Grace/Nana Grace

Acknowledgments

I wish to thank my editor, Donna Clark Goodrich, for all of the hours she spent editing the manuscript. She has been a faithful friend for many years. I also thank my Island Writers' Network associates for their help and advice when needed, and my daughter, Jessica, for her help in preparing the manuscript for publication.

Contents

Preface

From the time I was able to hold a pencil in my hand, I have loved to write. There is something magical about taking the twenty-six letters of our alphabet and creating words that people enjoy reading. Fiction or non-fiction, it makes no difference. We like to read about people and their lives. We are curious about how others live and cope, work and play, love and connect. Also, we like to learn new concepts for making our own lives better. Reading or listening to spoken words makes that possible.

In *Grace upon Grace*, a book about my journey of faith, I quoted Reverend Bud Robinson: "The reason it is so hard to make a book is that the maker is required to spread his brains out on paper."[1]

It takes thought, prayer, time, and experience to accomplish that task. Most books have been in the making for years before the words are committed to paper or typed on a keyboard.

On April 20, 1989, during my daily quiet time, the Lord revealed to me: "Your book will be a light unto the Gentiles.

You will be My spokesperson on grace. Others have written about it, but you are living it."

My reaction? Surely, I am not the only person God has called to talk about grace! And, of course, I am not. Many people have written about God's grace, but God also indicated I am "living it."

Kris Vallotton, senior associate leader at Bethel Church in Redding, California, has written, "Names can be prophetic declarations that define a person's identity. Great names can release power into our lives and bring us into our God-given destinies."[2]

In 1991, God gave further revelation of my destiny: "Grace is unconditional love. Grace-Grace has power in it. Your name has a double portion of grace. Wherever you go, people come under the conviction of the Holy Spirit. Be My messenger. Tell them, 'I love you.'"

Then He directed my thoughts to Zechariah 4:7: "What are you, O great mountain? Before Zerubbabel you will become a plain; and he will bring forth the top stone amid shouts of 'Grace, grace to it'!" The name Anne is derived from Hannah, meaning favored or gracious one, and Grace is my married name. Thus, "Grace-Grace" is my sword of the Spirit. Later, God gave me "A Song of Grace":

A song of grace is hovering in the air, Waiting to land within a grateful heart.

A song to heal, to comfort and deliver, Showing the love of God to all who hear.[3]

SONGS OF GRACE

Down through the ages, songs have expressed the feelings of people forever. We have the same hopes and dreams, fears and longings. Only God can meet our needs by His grace, so we must rely upon Him.

In this book, I have chosen to highlight five songs that express God's love and grace: "Amazing Grace," "'Twas Grace," "Rainbow of Grace," "Marvelous Grace," and "Only by Grace." Some are familiar hymns, and some are new ones God gave me. It is my desire that as you read this book or sing these songs, you will come to realize what a great, amazing, marvelous, loving God we serve, a God who wants to have a relationship with each of us. God is the instigator and the provider of love and grace. But first, we must believe Him and receive His Son Jesus's forgiveness and salvation. And we can only do this by His grace!

—Anne Sanders Grace

Amazing Grace

By John Newton (1725–1807)[4]

Amazing grace! how sweet the sound, That saved a wretch like me!

I once was lost, but now am found, Was blind, but now I see.

'Twas grace that taught my heart to fear, And grace my fears relieved;

How precious did that grace appear The hour I first believed!

Thro' many dangers, toils, and snares, I have already come;

'Tis grace hath bro't me safe thus far, And grace will lead me home.

The Lord has promised good to me, His word my hope secures;

He will my shield and portion be As long as life endures. AMEN.

Chapter 1

Amazing Grace

Grace hath put me in the number of the Savior's family.

—Abraham Lincoln

Following the massacre of nine men and women during a Bible study at Emanuel African Methodist Church in Charleston, South Carolina, in June 2015, the president of the United States, Barack H. Obama, spoke. At the close of his eulogy for the church pastor and South Carolina State Senator Clementa Pinckney, the president started singing the beloved hymn "Amazing Grace." Although his voice was somewhat shaky and he sang a little off-key, the organist quickly played in that tune and the choir sang with him. It was a very moving holy grace moment for all who witnessed it in person or by electronic media. That is what God's amazing grace is like. When we're uncertain about something or begin doing things the wrong way, God comes and makes it all right. God saves us from embarrassment and wrongdoing and gives us another chance to get our act together for eternity. He loves us and wants us to be like Him, doing good for those who need help. It is a sweet moment when we agree with God.

Several days after the memorial service, Leonard Pitts Jr., a journalist for the *Miami Herald*, wrote: "'As a nation, out of this terrible tragedy,' the president said, 'God has visited grace upon us, for he has allowed us to see where we've been blind. He's given us the chance, where we've been lost, to find our best selves.'"

LOST OR FOUND

At one point in time, each of us was lost and needed a Savior. Our eyes were blind to heaven's rewards, and we were headed in the wrong direction. But God, in His mercy and grace, found us and sent someone to show us the right path, such as a pastor, a teacher, a good friend, a spouse, or a parent.

John Newton's hymn "Amazing Grace" tells us about the "sweet sound that saved a wretch like me." Near Halloween, I once saw a *Family Circus* cartoon in which young Dolly is singing in church, "Amazing grace, how sweet the sound that saved a 'witch' like me." At times, we do feel like wretches or witches. When we've done wrong and need to make restitution, remorse sets in, and we feel awful.

FORGIVENESS

I vividly remember the time God impressed upon me to return items I had stolen in 1950 when I was a young girl. It happened in 1967 in an adult Sunday school class at a Methodist church in Sumter, South Carolina. By this time, I was married and pregnant with our second child. The teacher talked about doing things where we need to ask forgiveness. Suddenly, I heard an inaudible voice say to my spirit: *You have to give them back.* Immediately, I knew who was speaking and what He meant! When I was a child, I had stolen items from two friends in their homes. Now, seventeen years later, God wanted me to return them and ask forgiveness. I was afraid of rejection by my friends. But God's grace covered my fear as I obeyed. After I returned the first item, I felt God's cleansing power within my heart, as if a heavy burden had been lifted from my shoulders. My faith in God took a giant leap forward that day. God had a plan for my life, and I had to get rid of the dark stain of sin that had resided in my heart for years. Later I heard from one friend, "Of course I forgive you. We all do things as children that we shouldn't." Forgiveness is an oft overlooked grace. Sadly, it took two years to return the other item.

In the sermon on the Mount of Olives, Jesus told His disciples we must forgive, or God won't forgive us (Matthew 6:14–15). He also told the apostle Peter to forgive seventy times seven (Matthew 18:22), or each time throughout the day that we are asked to do so. We also have it in our power to forgive without being asked. In the Revelation to the apostle John, Jesus said, "Those whom I love, I reprove and discipline; be zealous therefore, and repent" (Revelation 3:19).

Author George Herbert (1593–1633) wrote, "He that cannot forgive others, breaks the bridge over which he himself must pass if he would ever reach heaven; for everyone has need to be forgiven."[5] Beloved author Mark Twain wrote, "Forgiveness is the fragrance the violet sheds

3

on the heel that has crushed it."[6] Another author, Marsha Marks, said it this way: "Grace is what we give to those who have just trashed what we value."[7] God's grace and forgiveness are equal parts of His character. Because of this, John Newton could sing, "'Twas grace that taught my heart to fear, and grace my fears relieved." He turned from doing wrong (slave trading) to doing what was right in God's sight (preaching, and writing more than 280 hymns). He was influenced by George Whitefield, and the Wesley brothers John and Charles, founders of Methodism. John Wesley's rules of conduct contain good advice for everyone:

> Do all the good you can,
> By all the means you can,
> In all the ways you can,
> In all the places you can,
> At all the times you can,
> To all the people you can,
> As long as ever you can.

THE LORD PROMISED GOOD

In 1985, our family moved from northern Virginia to a suburb of St. Louis, Missouri. We attended Salem-in-Ladue United Methodist Church, one block from our house. I joined the women's ministry and sang in the choir. Even though a person is actively involved serving God in a church, she may still question whether she is on the path God has chosen for her. One morning in April 1989, I prayed earnestly, seeking answers from God. I called God's telephone number, Jeremiah 33:3, which says, "Call to Me, and I will answer you, and I will tell you great and mighty things, which you do not know." As I cried out to God, I received this message:

My daughter, why weepest thou? I have called you to go and bear light to the nations that sit in darkness, the darkness of spiritual oppression. Your book will be a light unto the Gentiles. You will be My spokesperson on Grace. Others have written about it, but you are living it. You will go into all the world teaching and preaching by example. My Grace shall be poured out on all whom you serve.

Over the past thirty years, I have used this wisdom in all my activities of writing and speaking. I am always aware of God's grace in what I say and do. I know God loves me and has plans for my life. In 2000, I published a book about my journey of faith, *Grace upon Grace*, and I write monthly articles on the internet (www.annesgrace.com), sharing God's grace with my world.

On Friday, March 4, 2016, author Pat Conroy passed from this life into eternity. For two days, each time I read of his life and funeral in our local paper, I got goosebumps all over my body. Although I never met Pat, I saw him in person when he attended a speaking event of his wife, fellow author Cassandra King. I have read some of his books, especially the ones pertaining to the South. At his funeral, Cassandra followed the casket down the aisle as "Amazing Grace" played during the recessional. Outside the church, a lone bagpiper played the hymn, too. That reminded me of when my husband and I visited Scotland in 1992. Every day at eventide a bagpiper played "Amazing Grace" on a hilltop, as a gentle tribute to John Newton, and a closing prayer for the day.

Recently I found a newspaper article that mentions Cliff Barrows, who led choirs all over the world for decades at Billy Graham crusades. He said, "We will sing this song until

Jesus comes and it may be one of our theme songs in heaven around the throne."[8] It is only by God's grace, through faith and belief in Jesus, that we are able to accomplish what God has called each of us to do for others. His love and grace motivate me to keep obeying His call upon my life.

'Twas Grace

By Anne Sanders Grace (2006)[9]

'Twas Grace that loved me from the start.
'Twas Grace that changed my wayward heart.
Grace showed me how to love again When I had fallen into sin.

Chorus: Grace is coming again, One who forgave all my sin.
'Twas Grace that set me free To be all God planned for me.

'Tis Grace I need each and every day To help me walk in God's true way.
I look to God for all my cares, And Grace provides them through my prayers.

Chapter 2

'Twas Grace

God will channel His grace through you to bless others.

—Art Aragon

The song "'Twas Grace" was birthed in 2006 at a low point in my walk with God. He knew my faith needed to be strengthened. One morning, during my quiet time, the words and music flooded my spirit and my soul. I was overwhelmed by God's love and grace.

I have never doubted God's love for me, because I believe the Bible. However, I have done wrong things that caused God to look away from me. He won't look on sin, remember? Even Jesus cried, "My God! My God! Why have you deserted me?" as He hung on the cross for *our* sins! (See Matthew 27:46 CJB).

GRACE CHANGES HEARTS

The song says God's grace loved me from the start, and changed the way my heart was headed. The Bible tells us that God so loved the world, and everyone in it, that He gave (John 3:16). God is a giver! He withholds nothing good from those who believe in Him and return His love. God loved us before we even knew He existed. He allowed a sperm and a human egg to mate, creating the magnificent persons we are. Selah! Or as Costa Dier used to say, "What do you think about that!"

God loves me and created me in the womb with a problem (see Exodus 4:11). I was born with *pyloric stenosis,* a blockage from my stomach to my intestines. But God had a plan. A cousin had been born with the same problem, but no one in our small southwest Virginia town knew the solution, so he passed away at one month of age. When I evidenced the same symptoms at birth a year later in 1939, my mother and a nurse took me by train to Richmond, Virginia, where my father worked for the Virginia Department of Highways. After diagnosing the problem, Dr. John S. Horsley Jr. performed a new type of surgery. The procedure was later described in a Medical College of Virginia textbook. God uses some people to help fulfill His plans for others.

WALK IN TRUTH

As a child growing up in the Blue Ridge Mountains of Virginia, I eagerly looked forward to summer vacation at the beach. I am drawn to the ocean. I love walking on the beach, inhaling the fresh salt air and having the waves wash over my body. Although I grew up in the mountains, I am part

Only by Grace

ocean too—like God's grace and truth. The mountains are like truth, and the ocean represents grace. His love is grace, His word is truth, and His kingdom operates on both. Jesus is full of grace and truth, and He is coming back to earth. (John 1:14, 17; Revelation 22:20).

I now live on Hilton Head Island, South Carolina, and enjoy walking the beach whenever possible. At the beach, the tide turns twice each day. It brings in shells and sometimes seaweed, washing away filth from the sand. Graham Cooke has written, "In flood tide, many things are covered by the grace of God. In low tide, we discover ourselves as we really are and see God as He really is, all at the same time! His grace uncovers us so that we can be radically changed."[10] When God uncovers our sins before Him, it is not to embarrass us. It is to get us to repent and ask Him to forgive and blot it from memory—His and ours! We have all done wrong things we wish we had not done. When I am face to face with God at the end of my life and He reveals a playback of all I have done, I'll be glad my sins will all have been covered by the blood of Jesus. I would hate for my loved ones to see all the bad I have thought or done against others.

FALLEN INTO SIN

Sin is an ugly word. It reveals our baser instincts, the dark side of our soul. Most of us have been places and done things we later regretted. Oh, but for the grace of God! God's "grace becomes your fortress, your safe place that carries you through all the struggles of life," wrote Ruth Truman in her book *How to Be a Liberated Christian*.[11] We remember God, we thank Him for our protection, and His grace is poured out upon us. Often, we are unaware of it.

11

When we accept Jesus as our Savior and make Him Lord of our lives, our personal relationship with Him begins. What we say and do from that day on is counted either as righteousness or as dung. When we are in right standing with God, it is foolish to even think of doing wrong. And yet, we do. As I mentioned earlier, I stole items from friends, which God told me to return to the owners. I committed adultery. I have had to repent of many things and get back in God's good graces. All people on earth have strayed from God's plan, especially those who don't know God.

The Bible says *all* have sinned and fallen short of the glory of God (Romans 3:23). The Bible also says we have been saved through faith by God's gift of grace. No one can earn a gift; it is freely given (Ephesians 2:8). John Bevere asks, "Why are so many Christians living as they did before they were liberated by God's grace? Where is the disconnect?" He believes it is a lack of faith for not having "access to the grace that enables us to please God."[12] Pleasing God can only be done through grace.

GRACE IS COMING AGAIN

Please remember that Grace, the Lord Jesus Christ, is coming again. He forgives our sin when we confess it to Him, even though He knows all about it. He then sets us free to be what and whom He created us to do and be. The Bible also warns about people being cast into outer darkness, weeping and gnashing their teeth, because they are separated from the love and light of Christ (Matthew 13:41–42; Luke 13:28). These are people who thought they were true believers but realized they were Christian in name only! They may have followed church doctrine but not the way of Jesus. I hope those of you reading these words will not be among them. Because Jesus is coming again to rule and reign on earth in His kingdom, don't put off making things right with Him. In the last chapter of the last book of the Bible, Jesus says three times, "I am coming quickly" (Revelation 22:7, 12, 20). That can mean suddenly or without prior notice.

Stop reading this moment and ask God to forgive your sins. Tell Him you want to come into His kingdom of righteousness, peace, and joy! Then thank God for doing so. Record the date in a prominent place. Remember, God so loves *you* that He gave His Son Jesus to die physically so you won't have to die spiritually. Accept God's love, and love Him back! Then share that love with everyone you meet.

I was raised in the Methodist Church tradition. My maternal great-grandfather was a Methodist Circuit Rider in the Holston Conference of southwest Virginia and eastern Tennessee. I loved being in church, learning about Jesus in Sunday school, and singing in all the choirs. I even joined the church membership. But I wasn't really a Christian! So, I did foolish things, like stealing items from some friends. And yes, my parents had taught my sister, brother, and me right from wrong.

When I was thirteen years of age, God called me to accept Jesus as my Savior. In September of 1952, our town in southwest Virginia held a revival in one of the many tobacco warehouses. All the town churches combined to hire an evangelist, and the church choirs provided the worship music. Many young people attended during the week, because at that time we had no television, no internet, and no sports activities to interfere. On Saturday of that week, youth were invited to a special morning session. Several of us made a profession of faith in Jesus that day. Later, we were told to go home and write in our Bibles, "I was saved" and the date—September 22, 1952. That day, God's grace changed my wayward heart, and I began to serve my Lord in various ways. Ironically, ten years later, on that same date, I married Bobbie Lee Grace, prompting one of my aunts to say, "Oh, honey, you've been saved by grace!"

GOD'S WORDS

"'Twas grace that gave me words to say To help my friends to find God's way."

In 1990, my husband and I moved to Mesa, Arizona, where he worked at the McDonnell Douglas Helicopter Company. Being so far away from our families on the East Coast, I decided to write them monthly letters. Knowing most of them would get bored hearing what we were doing all the time, I chose to write it as *Goodnewsletter*, sharing my faith as well. For a couple of years, I snail-mailed typed messages to family and friends, telling them what God was revealing to me. Later, on a computer, I emailed the messages to those who chose to continue receiving them.

Several years ago, I opened a website (www.annesgrace.com) where I continue to post monthly articles. Often, the messages are "feel-good" ones, but sometimes they are hard to write and receive, for they hit too close to home, even to me. But I listen each day for what God wants people to hear, know, and try to understand. I continually need God's grace to help me write these words and be true to His calling. I pray for wisdom and guidance in all that I say and do. God speaks in His own way and time. Some days I observe what He is doing and saying through nature—animals, floods, fires, storms, quakes. Sometimes I hear the still small voice sharing with me. Often, it is through an article or a book I am reading.

Here are some words from others that have impacted my thinking:

- "It is the grace and favor of Heaven to set apart a people to be the beneficiaries and participants in the Father's great end-time plan." Bob Jones (*Shepherd's Rod*, 2002).
- "If you hesitate when God tells you to do a thing, you endanger your standing in grace." Oswald Chambers ("My Utmost for His Highest," May 10).
- "We live in a world that must have the grace and peace of God." Bobby Conner ("The Goals of Grace Provoke us to Reach Higher," 2008).
- "We are not only saved by grace, but we are given ability to overcome by His grace." John Belt ("Accessing His Grace by the Spirit," 2015).
- In his small book *Living in Dependency and Wonder*, author Graham Cooke wrote, "The grace of God helps us to feel good about our lives."

Also, God speaks through songs, especially ones He gives us. One such song He gave to me one morning involved a rainbow reflected in my kitchen. What a fantastic God I serve, who surprises me all the time with His messages!

Rainbow of Grace

By Anne Sanders Grace ©2014[13]

I'm dancing in the rainbow of the Lord,
Dancing in the rainbow of the Lord.
He pours out His grace when I look on His face,
I'm dancing in the rainbow of the Lord.

Chapter 3

Rainbow of Grace

We need to steal the rainbow back. It's a biblical sign anyway.

—Bishop Harry Jackson

Several years ago, I stood in my kitchen watching the colors of a rainbow appear on the white cabinet. I realized it came from a sun-catcher in the powder room window. It made me happy, so I danced around the room, and a song burst from my mouth:

> I'm dancing in the rainbow of the Lord,
> Dancing in the rainbow of the Lord.
> He pours out His grace when I look on His face,
> I'm dancing in the rainbow of the Lord.

Fun, frivolous, and free to enjoy God's love and grace!

In Genesis 6:8 we read, "Noah found favor [grace] in the eyes of the LORD." Noah and his family were the only righteous people found upon the earth at that time! Before God flooded the earth, He told Noah, "I will establish my covenant with you; and you shall enter the ark" (Genesis 6:18).

One of the reasons I chose a rainbow for the cover of this book is because of the promise God gave to Noah after the flood. "I set My bow in the cloud, and it shall be for a sign of a covenant between Me and the earth. I will remember My covenant which is between Me and you and every living creature of all flesh" (Genesis 9:13–15).

New York Times Journalist David Brooks wrote in a recent column in our local newspaper, *The Island Packet*: "A covenant exists between people who understand they are part of one another. It involves a vow to serve the relationship that is sealed by love." The dictionary defines covenant as "a binding agreement made by two or more individuals."[14] God gave the rainbow to Noah as a covenant of grace and a promise. Years later, God gave His beloved Son, Jesus, as a Covenant to all who would believe in and follow Him.

When we were children, we were told there was a pot of gold at the end of the rainbow. I suppose it is an Irish tale, because a leprechaun is usually pictured sitting on the pot of gold. So we childishly dreamed of finding the gold wherever the rainbow touched the ground following a rainstorm.

GOD'S RAINBOW

Today, the purpose of God's rainbow has become distorted. For some reason, the LGBTQ community has adopted the rainbow as a symbol for their liberated causes. The lesbian-gay lifestyle goes against the natural order of God's creation of male and female.

In the beginning, "God created man in His own image … male and female He created them" (Genesis 1:27). God put the man to sleep and took one rib from his side, forming a mate compatible for him, enclosing her with the same kind of flesh as his. God created humans both masculine and feminine within, although their body parts are different. The fall of man in the garden of Eden caused a distortion to arise where men began to prefer men instead of women. Satan was behind all this, perverting God's plan for men and women to multiply and replenish the earth with children, who would mature and do likewise. When two people of the same sex cohabitate, it is physically impossible for them to reproduce, thus wiping out a whole new generation of humans.

God created us the way we are, not necessarily the way we perceive ourselves. He loves His creation! When we get to heaven, we will no longer be sexual beings but spiritual beings, more like the angels.

CHOICES

The overwhelming characteristic of God is *love*! He loves everything and everyone He ever created. God wishes that all people would love Him in return. But some choose to walk in a different direction—away from God's presence. God gives us a choice. We are not puppets. He asks that we believe in Him and receive the promise of salvation through Jesus, who came to shed His blood and die on a cross in our place.

God loves the people who choose to become attracted to ones of their same sex. He will always love them. However, according to God's Word, they will not inherit the kingdom if they choose to remain in that lifestyle. In the book of Leviticus (18:22), God warned, "You shall not lie with a man as one does with a woman. It is an abomination" [loathing or odious or degrading habit or act].[15] The apostle Paul wrote to the people of Corinth,

> Do you not know that the unrighteous will not inherit the kingdom of God? Do not be deceived. Neither the sexually immoral, nor idolaters, nor adulterers, nor male prostitutes, nor homosexuals, nor thieves, nor covetous, nor drunkards, nor revilers, nor extortioners will inherit the kingdom of God. (1 Corinthians 6:9–10)

I realize this list includes more than the LGBTQ community. However, God is serious about what offends Him. If anyone is included here, consider how much God loves us to warn us to change our ways while we still have time.

We must understand that God is holy, and His kingdom consists of righteousness, peace, and joy in the Holy Spirit. Those who choose to be in right standing with God, who are in harmony with Him and are fellow believers, and who take delight in joyfully doing God's will are free to enter His kingdom.

In 2015, our US Supreme Court voted to allow marriage between any two consenting adults (homosexuals), not just a man and a woman. Although thousands of Christians prayed it would not be so, God chose to let it happen. After the signing into law of that decision, President Barak Obama allowed "the walls of the White House to be illumined in the colors of the rainbow, heaven's sacred sign," wrote Rabbi Jonathan Cahn. "The rainbow is a sacred vessel of God, a holy sign of His covenant. But we have now taken that sacred sign of covenant and desecrated it, using it as a vessel to desecrate the covenant of marriage" (*Charisma* magazine, June 2015). Also in that issue of *Charisma*, Jeremiah Johnson wrote what he believed God was saying: "In the natural, the Supreme Court justices have just legalized homosexual marriage in America, but little do they know that they also just authorized an awakening of the Spirit in My bride."

Lana Vawser, a prophet from Australia, confirmed that God "is the one who defines marriage, not a court system." She perceived God saying, "My Church is about to rise and shine like never before and show the nation of the United States what victory looks like." (*Charisma* magazine, July 2015).

HE POURS OUT GRACE

Because of the success in getting people to recognize the basic LGBTQ lifestyle, transgender individuals are revealing their choices too, including people we idolize in the news. The liberal media has made it appear as if this is the new norm today. Personally, I only know of one male who changed from being a husband and father to wanting to be recognized and accepted as a female.

The issue of male and female restrooms being used by both sexes has affected several state governments here in our nation, even involving lawsuits. This attempt exploded exponentially over the last few months of 2016. Is the

USA so bewitched by sex and gender that we can't think rationally? Recently, I read about a little boy who had been dressed and treated as a girl for years, and the child is now in kindergarten wanting to use the girls' restroom. Does he really *believe* he is a female, or have his parents caused him to behave this way?

The truth is God loves all homosexual and transgender people, because He created them. He showers His grace upon them also. But maybe they don't care to know who God is or what He thinks! Some people say it doesn't matter, that God's grace covers it all. That is known as "cheap grace." Maxie D. Dunnam calls that "soft religion without any muscle of responsibility and demand for moral conduct and commitment to righteousness."[16] John Belt of Overflow Global Ministries says, "God's grace is meant to bring us up higher. His grace is not a license to live in an inferior place of sin and self-justification for acts of unrighteousness."[17] In "The Cost of Discipleship," Dietrich Bonhoeffer wrote, "Cheap grace is the preaching of forgiveness without repentance, baptism without church discipline, communion without confession, absolution without personal confession. Cheap grace is grace without Jesus Christ, living and incarnate."[18] And Lance Wallnau wrote in an article in *Charisma* magazine October 2016, "Common grace is the grace of God that comes down upon a fallen world to keep in check the forces of anarchy, and the inclination of the sinful nature of man to self-destruct."[19]

The apostle Paul advised the people in Colossae, "Set your mind on the things above, not on the things that are on earth … immorality, impurity, passion, evil desires, and greed … For it is on account of these things that the wrath of God will come" (Colossians 3:2–6). Twice in the book of Luke, Jesus said, "Unless you repent, you will all likewise perish" (Luke 13:3, 5). Our relationship with Jesus is more important than any other we have here on earth. Our future is with Him if we have accepted Jesus as our Lord and Savior. When our physical body dies, our spirit and soul will live on somewhere in eternity—in heaven or in hell—so the Bible tells us. While alive, we still have a choice of where we will end up. Let's choose wisely.

Most Christians pray, "Thy kingdom come. Thy will be done on earth as it is in heaven." God is bringing His kingdom to earth for those who have prepared for it.

Dancing around my kitchen that day and singing, "He pours out His grace when I look on His face," reminds me all I have to do is look at God each day and be aware of His love for me and all humankind. Have you looked in God's face lately to realize how holy and full of grace He is? His grace is too marvelous to comprehend, but we need it if we expect to enter the kingdom when Jesus returns.

Grace Greater Than Our Sin

By Julia H. Johnston (c. 1910)[20]

Marvelous grace of our loving Lord, Grace that exceeds our sin and our guilt!

Yonder on Calvary's mount outpoured—There where the blood of the Lamb was spilt.

Chorus: Grace, grace, God's grace, Grace that will pardon and cleanse within;

Grace, grace, God's grace, Grace that is greater than all our sin!

Dark is the stain that we cannot hide, What can avail to wash it away?

Look! There is flowing a crimson tide—Whiter than snow you may be today.

Marvelous, infinite, matchless grace, Freely bestowed on all who believe!

You that are longing to see His face, Will you this moment His grace receive?

Chapter 4

Marvelous Grace

Love, faith and wisdom will get you on base,
but only My grace can get you home.

—Bob Jones (from a dream about baseball)

OUR LOVING LORD

Always remember, God loves you. That is the most
important statement anyone needs to hear and understand.
God loves all that He created—the universe, our earth, the
animals, and human beings. Whether or not you know God
personally, He sent His Son Jesus to convey love to you. And
that, my friends, is marvelous grace!

Remember the first time your friend, lover, mate, or
spouse said, "I love you"? Did you feel special? Like you were
accepted and cherished? When that one person indicated

you were precious and loveable? Did you return the love? Was this the special person you had looked for in life?

Now, consider how God's love makes you feel or think. Is the spiritual part of your being as excited as the physical is with your soulmate? Of course, God's love is different from sexual feelings and emotions but no less powerful. God doesn't just love and accept us; He also forgives our wrongdoings, our sins against Him and against our fellow beings. That is known as *grace*.

GRACE PARDONS

God's grace pardons and cleanses us on the inside because God took away our sin and guilt when Jesus shed His blood for us on that Roman cross over two thousand years ago. In her hymn, "Grace Greater Than Our Sin," Julia H. Johnson wrote: "Look! There is flowing a crimson tide," and she did not mean the University of Alabama football team! God let His Son suffer for the sin of the whole world even though some people refuse to acknowledge God or accept Jesus as their Savior (see John 3:16–17). God did it then so we could say yes to Him today. God's grace is greater than all our sin—past, present, or future.

Sin threatens our soul by separating us from God's presence. God cannot look on sin, even turning His back on Jesus when He took our sin upon His body during the crucifixion. God is light, and separation from Him is darkness. Most of us have experienced a "dark night of the soul" in our life. A time where everything appeared to go wrong, and nothing seemed right. Where we lost all hope of things returning to normal.

I remember such a time in 1976. I had invested a year getting to know a woman who appeared more spiritual than I. We "did lunch" together, prayed for our families and friends, shared Scriptures, and enjoyed being together doing God's will, or so we thought. However, gradually things changed. God began to open my eyes to what was happening. I liken it to a spider and a fly. Once, a spider rested on our back porch screen door. A fly walked on the screen, not aware of the spider. When the fly got too close, the spider jumped the fly and wrapped it with a sticky substance. I felt like I had been drawn into this spiritual person's web and couldn't escape.

The apostle Paul wrote in his letter to the church in Corinth, "No temptation has overtaken you but such as is common to man; and God is faithful, who will not allow you to be tempted beyond what you are able, but with the temptation will provide the way of escape also, that you may be able to endure it" (1 Corinthians 10:13).

Edward Mote penned words in the hymn "Solid Rock," which also advises, "When darkness veils his lovely face, I rest on his unchanging grace." By God's grace and His word, I was able to move on again from that relationship. But it took a toll on my life and that of my family. Many days later, I asked God to forgive me, and then I forgave her and prayed for God to forgive and restore her to Himself. (I wrote about this experience in *Grace upon Grace*, my journey of faith.)

DARK STAIN

That period was a dark stain on my soul. Most humans have one at some point in life. How great to know all we have to do is ask, "God, forgive?" and God does. It gets washed away by the shed blood of Jesus. For that I am grateful!

FREELY BESTOWED

God freely bestows grace on all who believe in Him and obey His words. I find it interesting that the Bible says one day we will all stand at the judgment seat of God to give an account of our deeds done on earth (see Romans 14:10, 12). We will be face to face with our Creator. If we hope to hear God say, "Well done," we must receive His grace.

The last verse in Julia Johnston's hymn says God's grace is *marvelous, infinite, matchless. The Reader's Digest Oxford Complete Word Finder*[21] defines *marvelous* as "astonishing; excellent; extremely improbable." Yeah, God's grace is like that! It is also *infinite,* meaning "boundless; endless." Another way of saying that would be "forever." God's love, mercy, and grace are forever, infinite. The third word Julia used is *matchless,* meaning "without an equal, incomparable; unique." No human being could bestow upon us these attributes, only God the Father. He bestows grace upon grace to all who believe in Him, who acknowledge Jesus as Lord and Savior. "And the Word became flesh, and dwelt among us, and we beheld His glory … full of grace and truth" (John 1:4), or as *The Message* says, "The Word became flesh and blood, and moved into the neighborhood" (John 1:4 MSG).

RECEIVING GRACE

When we kneel at the foot of the cross, we find grace, who is Jesus the Christ. There we receive salvation and allow His Spirit to indwell us, teaching how to live His life through us. If we are sincere, we will follow the path God has chosen and revealed to us. E. Stanley Jones wrote in *The Way,* "Grace is free, but when once you take it you are bound forever to the Giver, and bound to catch the spirit of the Giver."[22]

What is your passion? What really excites and energizes you? What do you enjoy doing above all else? My passion is reading, then writing. I journal my thoughts and plans every day. I also love to cook, swim, and walk, but I'd rather read than anything else! My bookshelves are full of invisible friends. Some of their advice I have taken, and some has fallen by the wayside. But I have been changed by reading their thoughts and deeds. Some of my favorite authors are Catherine Marshall, Marjorie Holmes, Sue Monk Kidd, Annie Dillard, Perry Stone, Bill Johnson, Fuschia Pickett, Anne Lamont, Rick Joyner, Graham Cooke, and Maya Angelou. I also have a shelf full of books about grace from which I glean insight about God's message of grace through those authors. A few examples:

- "Grace is like grits. You don't order it. It just comes." M. Scott Peck[23]
- "If it isn't amazing, it isn't grace." David Redding[24]
- "Happiness is the spiritual experience of living every minute with love, grace and gratitude." Denis Waitley[25]
- "Sometimes grace works like waterwings when you feel as if you are sinking." Anne Lamott[26]

Years ago, God revealed this to me: "The door to the Kingdom of Grace will always be open ... until the Bridegroom comes and shuts it. Then it will be too late to enter" (see Matthew 25:10).

Gerritt Gustafson, author of the beautiful song "Only By Grace," says it very plainly. Only by God's grace can we enter His kingdom. Period. God pours out His grace on everyone, but not all will receive it. How sad to think some of the people we love will not be with us in eternity, because they never said, "Yes, Lord."

Only by Grace

Gerritt Gustafson (c. 1990)[27]

Only by grace can we enter Only by grace can we stand
Not by our human endeavor But by the blood of the
Lamb

Into Your presence You call us You call us to come
Into Your presence You draw us And now by Your grace
we come

Lord, if You marked our transgressions Who would
stand
Thanks to Your grace we are cleansed by the blood of
the Lamb
Lord, if You marked our transgressions Who would
stand
Thanks to Your grace we are cleansed by the blood of
the Lamb.

Chapter 5

Only by Grace

Let the word of Christ richly dwell within you, with all wisdom teaching and admonishing one another with psalms and hymns and spiritual songs, singing with thanksgiving [grace] in your hearts to God.

—Apostle Paul (Colossians 3:16)

ONLY BY GRACE

It is only by grace that we can enter God's kingdom. Some people will say that statement is too confining; there are many ways to God, to salvation, to heaven, or wherever they hope to end up. God gives each of us a choice—to believe His words or to go our own way. *We* choose!

In Jesus's conversation with Nicodemus, He spoke words that are very familiar to most people: "For God so loved the world, that He gave His only begotten Son, that whoever believes in Him should not perish, but have eternal life" (John 3:16). In his book *The Grace Factor*, Barry Cook wrote, "You see, grace is not a thing; it is a *person*."[28] God wants us to believe in Jesus and what He did for us while He lived here on earth. Also, God wants us to understand what Jesus is doing for us in Heaven. Regardless of what we have done, He still loves us and intercedes for us on a daily basis! God wants us to become reunited with Him someday— soon, we hope.

WE ENTER

This song says we enter God's Kingdom through grace. In his book *Grace Is Not a Get Out of Hell Free Card*, Steve Foss wrote, "Grace is the favor of God that gives us access to the power of God for everything we need for life and godliness."[29] We all need God's grace.

The apostle Peter wrote, "Grace and peace be multiplied to you in the knowledge of God and of Jesus our Lord" (2 Peter 1:2–3). We must come to really know God and Jesus, and establish a relationship with them while the door to the kingdom is still open. Grace is a gift which God bestows upon us until we say yes to Him and His salvation. The apostle Paul taught we are saved by grace through faith in Jesus (see Ephesians 2:8). Later, Peter exhorts us to "grow in the grace and knowledge of our Lord and Savior Jesus Christ" (2 Peter 3:18). We grow this way by studying the Bible, by praying to God, and by listening to what God says. Maxie D. Dunnam, in a commentary about the book of Galatians, wrote, "The true children of Abraham, the true inheritors of the Promise, are ... those who have been set spiritually free by the grace of Jesus Christ."[30] The apostle Peter also wrote, "The Lord is not slow about His promise … but is patient toward you, not wishing for any to perish but for all to come to repentance" (2 Peter 3:9).

Jesus taught His disciples about the kingdom that is to come. "Enter by the narrow gate. For the gate is small, and the way is narrow that leads to life, and few are those who find it" (Matthew 7:13–14). The narrow gate is sort of like the road less traveled, about which M. Scott Peck wrote. We do not have to become nuns or monks in order to find the narrow way. But we do need to become more aware of our relationship with Jesus. He loves us and wants to spend quality time with us, as we do with our spouse or fiance'(e) or our children.

Jesus also taught about the wide gate. "For the gate is wide, and the way is broad that leads to destruction, and many are those who enter by it" (Matthew 7:13). The wide gate entices us to do things that go against the will of God. Too many activities—like watching certain TV programs, X-rated movies, internet porn, excessive sports, or racy magazines and books—can lead us astray.

Although we don't like to read about God's *do nots*, He gave them as guidelines or boundaries for our lives. God's "Big Ten" is not a football conference! He set specific rules for godly living (see Exodus 20:3–17).

1. No other gods but Me.
2. No idols.
3. Don't speak God's name in vain. (No cursing with it!)
4. Honor the Sabbath day as holy.
5. Honor your parents.
6. Do not murder.

7. Do not commit adultery. (No fornication either!)
8. Do not steal.
9. Do not slander your neighbor. (No gossip!)
10. Do not covet your neighbor's belongings.

Some may say, "But that was Old Testament stuff!" I ask, "Is there any truth there *not* valid for today?"

God also set boundaries for those of us who live under the New Covenant. Because He loves us, God gave revelation to Paul in his letter to the Galatians (and to us) warning or advising or instructing:

> Now the deeds of the flesh are evident, which
> are: immorality, impurity, sensuality, idolatry,
> sorcery, enmities, strife, jealousy, outbursts
> of anger, disputes, dissensions, factions,
> envying, drunkenness, carousing, and things
> like these, of which I forewarn you … those
> who practice such things shall not inherit the
> kingdom of God. (Galatians 5:19–21)

People who indulge in these ungodly activities have entered the wide gate Jesus talked about, the one that leads to destruction, not to His kingdom. (Note: it says "those who *practice* such things," not those who may have sinned in one area at any one time.)

Jesus taught His disciples to pray, "Thy kingdom come." But what is God's kingdom like? Jesus gave many examples recorded by Matthew, Mark, Luke, and John: it's for the poor in spirit; it's the good seed sown; sowed mustard seed; leaven hidden in meal; treasure hidden in a field; merchant seeking fine pearls; dragnet cast into the sea; king who gave a wedding feast for his son; and five of the ten virgins who went out to meet the bridegroom. Jesus reminded us, "Many are called, but few are chosen" (Matthew 22:14). Not everyone who is invited into the kingdom will choose to come. How sad!

The Psalmist, probably King David, had written and sung this advice to all who would hear: "Enter His gates with thanksgiving, And His courts with praise. Give thanks to Him; bless His name. For the LORD is good; His lovingkindness [grace] is everlasting, and His faithfulness to all generations" (Psalm 100:4–5). As we enter the kingdom and the presence of God, we will give Him thanks and praise. That is the offering God expects from us. A pretty neat exchange for His grace, I believe!

When Jesus returns and separates the nations as sheep and goats, He will say to the sheep on His right, "Come, you who are blessed of My Father, inherit the kingdom prepared for you from the foundation of the world" (Matt 25:34). They are the nations who fed the hungry and thirsty, invited in strangers, clothed the naked, and visited those in prison, as doing it unto the Lord Jesus. Today, we would include those who have soup kitchens, support halfway houses, hold clothing giveaways, and employ prison chaplains.

WE STAND

There is an old church hymn written by Russell Kelso Carter in 1885:

> Standing on the promises of Christ my King,
> Through eternal ages let His praises ring,
> Glory in the highest I will shout and sing,
> Standing on the promises of God.[31]

Carter was a professor, writer, musician, minister, and a doctor. He made great use of all the gifts and talents God bestowed on him. How many of us today stand on even *one* promise from God? Whatever God has called and gifted us to do, we need to be diligent about finishing it. Time as we know it is running out! Jesus will return soon, and we must be doing what He gave us to do until He arrives. Jesus once told His disciples, "Occupy until I come" (Luke 19:13). Even if I don't get this book finished and published before He appears in the sky, at least I will be occupied writing it!

By God's grace, we will be able to do what He has assigned for us. In the Bible, we are exhorted: Stand forth; stand up, stand fast; stand in prayer; stand and gird your loins with truth; stand in grace. Even Jesus stands at the door of believers' hearts and knocks, waiting for us to open and let Him in (see Revelation 3:20). He wants to become intimate with us because he loves us.

In Paul's letter to the Romans, he wrote, "Through our Lord Jesus Christ ... we have obtained our introduction by faith into this grace in which we stand, and we exult [be in high spirits and glory before God] in hope of the glory of God" (Romans 5:2). So, we stand, we sing, we praise, and we hope for His soon return. Because of the shed blood of the Lamb for those who believe, God will not mark our transgressions. Jesus's blood has cleansed us from our faults because of God's grace.

YOU CALL US

The song "Only by Grace" says, "Into Your presence You call us, You call us to come. Into Your presence You draw us, And now by Your grace we come." Paul wrote to those saints who are faithful in Christ Jesus, "For by grace you have been saved through faith; and that not of yourselves, it is the gift of God; not as a result of works, that no one should boast" (Ephesians 2:8–9). When we believe in God, we enter the realm of faith. We learn to trust God and rely on His promises and His plans for our lives. Grace is a gift from God, not based on anything we have done or will do. God looked down through eternity and saw those who believed Him and chose us to follow Jesus. In his devotional book *My Utmost for His Highest,* Oswald Chambers wrote, "'I have chosen you.' That is the way the grace of God begins. The drawing is done by the supernatural grace of God."[32]

The song continues to say that if the Lord marked our transgressions, we would not be able to stand before Him. But "thanks to Your grace we are cleansed by the blood of the Lamb." There is another old hymn written by Robert Lowry:

> What can wash away my sin?
> Nothing but the blood of Jesus;
> What can make me whole again?
> Nothing but the blood of Jesus.[33]

In writing to the Ephesians about Jesus, Paul said, "In Him we have redemption through His blood, the forgiveness of our trespasses, according to the riches of His grace" (Ephesians 1:7). Jesus, who is full of grace and truth, calls us, cleanses us, and uses us. It's all about His grace, and He is coming again.

Because this is a kingdom message, we need to heed the words of the writer to the Hebrews:

> Therefore, since we receive a kingdom
> which cannot be shaken, let us show

gratitude, by which we may offer to God an acceptable service with reverence and awe; for our God is a consuming fire. (Hebrews 12:28–29)

When we receive a gift from someone, we use it and enjoy it. When we receive a gift from God, we are expected to share it. One of my gifts is writing God's messages, which I gladly share with those who wish to receive them. May all who read these words be blessed by our Father God and our Savior Jesus Christ. He is full of grace and offers it to us for eternity in His kingdom.

May the grace of the Lord Jesus be with all. AMEN.

—Revelation 22:21

Anne Sanders Grace

Notes

Preface:

1. Bud Robinson, *Sunshine and Smiles* (Noblesville, IN: Newby Books, 1973), p. 111
2. Kris Vallotton, *The Supernatural Ways of Royalty* (Destiny Image; Shippensburg, PA; 2006), p.64
3. Anne Sanders Grace, "A Song of Grace" sung to tune Finlandia; April 2010

Chapter 1: Amazing Grace

4. "Amazing Grace" by John Newton (1725–1807), (The Methodist Hymnal, c. 1932, 1935, 1939; The Methodist Book Concern, Nashville, TN), p.209
5. George Herbert, *The Encyclopedia of Religious Quotations* (Spire Books, 1976), p.222
6. Mark Twain, *The Encyclopedia of Religious Quotations* (Spire Books, 1976), p.226
7. Marsha Marks, *101 Amazing Things About God* (Tulsa, OK: River Oaks Publishing, 2001)
8. Cliff Barrows, "How Enduring the Sound" article by Joe Edwards, The Island Packet, Nov 20,2010

Chapter 2: 'Twas Grace

9. "'Twas Grace" by Anne Sanders Grace (c. 2006)
10. L. Graham Cooke, email June 2000
11. Ruth Truman, *How To Be A Liberated Christian* (Nashville, TN: Abingdon Press, 1981), p.156
12. John Bevere, *Grace: The Big Disconnect* (Internet Article, Charismamag.com, 30 March 2010)

Chapter 3: Rainbow of Grace

13. "Rainbow of Grace" by Anne Sanders Grace (c. 2014)
14. "Covenant", *Concordance to the New American Standard Bible* (Nashville, TN: Thomas Nelson, Inc., 1985), p.16
15. "Abomination", *Reader's Digest Oxford Complete Word Finder* (Pleasantville, NY: The Reader's Digest Association, Inc., 1993), p.324
16. Maxie D. Dunnam, *Communicators Commentary* (Nashville, TN: WORD BOOKS, Book of Ephesians, 1982), p.207
17. John Belt, Overflow Global Ministries; quote from "Removing the Leaven From Our Lives"; 11 April 2013 (from website)
18. Dietrich Bonhoeffer, "The Cost of Discipleship"; (c. 1959; TOUCHSTONE, New York, NY; pp. 44–45).
19. Lance Wallnau, *Charisma* magazine, October 2016

Chapter 4: Marvelous Grace

20. "Grace Greater than Our Sin" by Julia H. Johnston (c. 1910; Renewal 1938 Hope Publishing Co., *Hymns for the Family of God*, Paragon Associates, Inc., Nashville, TN, 1976)
21. *Reader's Digest Oxford Complete Word Finder* (Pleasantville, NY: The Reader's Digest Association, Inc.,1993), p. 919 "marvelous"; p. 763 "infinite"; p. 923 "matchless"

22. E. Stanley Jones, *The Way* (Nashville, TN: Abingdon-Cokesbury Press, 1946)
23. M. Scott Peck, *The Road Less Travelled & Beyond* (Touchstone 1997), p.157
24. David Redding, *Amazed By Grace* (F H Revell, 1986)
25. Denis Waitley, www.brainyquote.com
26. Anne Lamott, *GRACE (Eventually) Thoughts On Faith* (New York, NY: Riverhead Books, Penguin Group, 2007), p.50

Chapter 5: Only By Grace

27. "Only By Grace" by Gerritt Gustafson (c. 1990), Integrity's Hosanna! Music (ASCAP), Capital CMG Publishing.com
28. Barry Cook, *The Grace Factor* (Honor Net, 2006), p.7
29. Steve Foss, *GRACE Is Not A Get Out of Hell Free Card* (Charisma House Publishing, 2013)
30. Maxie D. Dunnam, (Communicators Commentary, Word Publisher, Vol 8, 1982), p.95
31. Russell Kelso Carter (1849–1926), "Standing On The Promises" (Published in *Songs of Perfect Love*, 1886)
32. Oswald Chambers, *My Utmost For His Highest* (New York, NY: Dodd, Mead & Company, Inc., 1935), p.269
33. Robert Lowry (1826–1899), "Nothing But The Blood", *Baptist Hymnal* (Nashville, TN: Convention Press, 11956), p. 204

Printed in the United States
By Bookmasters